BULGARIAN MYTHOLOGY & LEGENDS

Journey Through Time with Myths and Folklore

CHRONICLE PRESS

Disclaimer

The author is solely responsible for this book's information, ideas, and opinions; they do not necessarily represent the views of any organizations, institutions, or individuals associated with the author. The author has made what they believe to be reasonable steps to make sure that the material contained in this book is accurate. However, neither the author nor the publisher makes any representations or guarantees, either stated or implied, regarding the completeness, accuracy, reliability, appropriateness, or availability of the content contained within. It is strongly recommended that readers seek assistance from relevant professionals or specialists in specific disciplines by consulting with them to acquire precise information tailored to their particular situations. The author disclaims liability for any loss, damage, or harm resulting from using the information provided in this book and any omissions or errors.

This book may reference websites, goods, services, or resources owned or operated by third parties. These references are solely offered for your convenience, and their inclusion does not indicate that we approve, sponsor, or recommend the content provided by the third party. Because the author and the publisher do not have any control over the nature, content, or availability of external websites, they cannot be held liable for any actions, decisions, or consequences resulting from using such external resources.

Forward

I would want to extend an invitation to go on a voyage that is genuinely extraordinary to those of you who are interested in unearthing ancient knowledge, who are captivated by the mysterious stories that are woven through the fabric of human life, and who are aficionados of the rich tapestry of mythology that transcends boundaries and resonates across time. Within this book's covers, we will explore the halls of myth and completely submerge ourselves in the ageless tales that have enthralled the human imagination for as long as anybody can remember.

In all of its magnificence, mythology acts as a compass that directs us through the complexities of the human experience. It is a mirror that reflects our perception of the universe and our role and embodies our collective dreams, fears, goals, and ideals. Mythology invites us to investigate the hidden aspects of our lives, whether we are more interested in the sweeping conflicts between gods and heroes or the hidden meanings in the stories of how the world was created.

Within these pages, you will encounter many pantheons and deities, each providing a distinctive perspective to examine the more expansive universe. As we delve deeper into these enthralling tales, it is essential to remember that mythology is not only a relic of the past but a living phenomenon that continues to impact our contemporary reality. Its influence can be seen in literature, art, music, and daily language. It invigorates us, sparks the fire of our imagination, and gives us a glimpse into the intricate web that is the history of humanity.

Mythology also acts as a connector, bringing together people from different cultures worldwide. It brings us together by highlighting the similarities in our experiences and the uniqueness of each of us as individuals. In the vast pantheon of mythical figures, we find examples of universal themes such as love, betrayal, heroism, and sacrifice. These themes connect with every human heart, regardless of when or where they were written.

This book is both a celebration of mythology and an invitation to go on an adventure of discovery. This is a homage to the innumerable storytellers who have ensured the survival of these myths through the ebb and flow of the sands of time by passing them down from generation to generation. It is devoted to all people interested in mythology, namely those who find comfort in the ageless stories that have shaped our world since the beginning of time and continue to do so today.

Therefore, I implore you, dear reader, to turn the page and completely submerge yourself in the enthralling delights that are still to come. Let us all come together to celebrate the mythology that brings us together that is not limited by the constraints of culture or time, and imparts a feeling of awe and wonder into our everyday lives.

Your imagination will be stoked, your horizons will be expanded, and you will be reminded of the eternal power of storytelling if you allow yourself to go on this voyage into the realms of mythology. And may you emerge from these pages, like the heroes of old, changed by the insight and enchantment that mythology has to give due to what you've learned here.

TABLE OF CONTENTS

CHAPTER 1: INTRODUCTION

The history of Bulgaria is intricate and replete with a wide variety of tales and legends concerning beings and people. Most of these tales and legends have a Slavic heritage, yet some originate from other ethnic groups. Myths and tales in Bulgaria have been enriched as a result of the country's diverse cultural and ethnic backgrounds, which has resulted in Bulgarian mythology being one of several types in the realm of the Slavs.

Folk tales from Bulgaria are known for their stark, natural themes, simple literary beauty, and archetypal solid characters. The characters are larger than life. They are epic heroes, warrior women, and mysterious beings who live in a fantasy world with its own rules, laws, and logic. They have many levels and show ancient roots, possibly going back to the time of the Thracians and even further. Greece, Thrace, and the Proto-Bulgarians were the three main groups living in what is now Bulgaria. The country is at the intersection of the East and West. These groups of people used to be separate and ethnically different, with very different religions and cultures. This mix has made Bulgaria's history-rich, and its folklore and customs are still alive today.

The old Thracians were an Indo-European tribe that lived in the area within the Balkans that is now the country of Bulgaria. They moved there at least five thousand years ago. They were great at breeding horses, growing great vines and wines, and working with metal in a very artistic way, making beautiful jewellery, religious items, and vessels. Their society was just as prosperous as the Greeks, but they lacked written language. We know a lot about them because of the Greek writers who lived at the same time as them and the many artefacts that have been found.

The Thracians were very religious. They worshipped the sun and thought that the soul could live forever. In Thracian legend, The myths and culture of Thrace are intense, going from light to dark. The place is in a wild mountainous area where a great goddess hunts, horses are holy, and the enigmatic Thracian Horseman deals with life and death. Orpheus, a legendary singer, musician, healer, and magician, goes down to the Underworld to find Eurydice, his dead wife and promises her that she will live forever and be born again.

After the sixth century AD, the Slavic and Bulgarian people there swallowed the Thracians. However, their traditions were passed on to the next Bulgarian kingdom. Archaeological finds from the Thracian period can be found all over Bulgaria. Thracian faith and mythology can still be seen in Bulgarian folklore and traditions, like the ones below.

Saluti Samodivi Many stories are told about these strange female nymphs that live in water, forests, and mountains. They are known for singing and dancing very beautifully. Most people think they are Slavic, but in Bulgarian myth, they are similar to the Thrace goddess Bendis in some ways. In one story, Vida, a strong samodiva from the Pirin mountains, mounts a stag while holding a bow and carrying arrows on her back. The grass snakes that hold her reins and her whip are also snakes. She runs away to the moon and kills the handsome male singer Ivo. Then, she brings him back to life on the healing grounds of Magda Samovila. Some stories say that Samodivi can call the moon down and milk it like a cow. In some stories, they kill or remove the heads of people who cross them, which makes me think of the Maenads, Dionysus's happy female followers who ripped Orpheus apart when they were drunk.

The great Hero Krali Marko riding his horse Sharkoliya There was a natural person named Krali Marko who thrived in the 1400s AD. He is now mixed with older stories similar to the Thracian Horseman, the divine, sometimes called Hero. Stories about Krali Marko's stories with his magic horse Sharkoliya were traditionally told through songs. There are many songs about these experiences. Orpheus is a model for Bulgaria's old style of singing, which is known all over the globe for its haunting voices and beautiful harmonies. Some people also think Bulgarian music's strange, uneven beats may come from Thrace.

The Slavs moved to the Balkan area in Central Europe during the early 700s AD. They believed in many gods, nature spirits, and devils and saw supernatural forces and energies around them. They were an agricultural people who loved freedom and lived in democratic clan communes without strict rules or orders. Witches, vampires, werewolves, and water and wood nymphs are some of them. People worshipped rivers, trees, and animals as if they were ancestors. Fire and the sun were essential to cult activities, and seasonal festivals were a big part of their religion.

The Slavs worshipped their gods as statues in shrines. The god of thunder, Perun, was their most important god. The Pirin Mountains in southern Bulgaria are named after him. Those with horns were blessed by Volos, also written as Veles. Lada and Lyulya, gods of love and nature waking, were two less important female gods. The Ladouvane is An event for girls that gets its name to Lada, a Slavic goddess for love. It is part of a tradition called "the song of the bell rings" to tell people their futures. Traditional Bulgarian bridal songs also talk about the goddess.

People who are vampires This is one among multiple Slavic monsters. Not following the right ways to bury and honour the dead can cause the dead to come back to life as vampires that walk around at night, taking blood from people and animals and suffocating people who are sleeping. Vampires can be made when someone or something jumps over a dead body when the body isn't correctly washed, when the dead person isn't adequately mourned, or when someone dies violently. A Bulgarian story says that a vampire's bite doesn't spread disease and has nothing to do with bats.

Some say that vampires look like shapeless sacks of

blood for the first forty days of their lives. After that, they get sufficiently robust to form bones and take on a human shape. Afterwards, they can come out of the tomb during the day, get employment, and possibly get married. They must be careful never to harm themselves, though, or they will explode and turn into a pool of gooey blood.

Putting hot oil in the grave, hawthorn or blackberry, fire, a nail, a stake, or a silver bullet are some of the many ways to kill a vampire. Also, everyone knows that vampires are stupid and not very smart. For instance, if you sent one to get fish from the Danube, he would fall in and die.

It's not clear where the Proto-Bulgarians came from. However, it was possibly the Altai Mountains in Central Asia or the northernmost part of China. In the past, the Proto-Bulgarians were nomads who kept herds and respected horses. The milk from mares was an essential part of their food. They were great fighters and had well-organized armies. They were also good at working with metal and inhabited clans led by Khans, who had complete power. In return for keeping the local Slavs safe from Byzantine attack, they set up the first Bulgarian kingdom in the Balkans in 681 AD.

Their faith was based on the sun and light, and Tangra, the sky god, was their most important god. The mount and the eagle were sacred to Tangra. People loved white horses the most. The Proto-Bulgarians didn't have a writing system, but they did have their calendar. It was based on a 12-year cycle, such as the Chinese calendar, and each year was named after an animal, bird, or lizard. There was shamanism, and every family had a holy animal totem. Wolves, dogs, and deer seem to have been especially important.

It's safe to say that Bulgaria is a mystery, given its long past and the many ethnic groups that live there now. But the variety has helped make a world of myths and folktales that are both unique and related to other Slavic stories told around the world. The first thing we must know about Bulgarian folk is that most myths and tales about these creatures occur in a village or on a mountain. Bulgaria has many mountains. As you might expect from old Slavic stories, other creatures can be found in people's homes or graveyards. Now, without further ado, let's talk about the most well-known animals in Bulgarian mythology and folklore.

CHAPTER 2: GODS AND HEROS

In mythology, gods are strong and often mystical beings important to different cultures' beliefs, stories, and customs. Most of the time, these divine beings are shown to have unique powers, like shaping the world, affecting natural events, and deciding people's fates. In different countries and times, gods represent different things, like wisdom, strength, love, and even mischief. They are the main characters in myths, legends, and religious stories.

People study the stories and tales about the gods to figure out their role in explaining the unidentified, teaching moral lessons, and keeping society in order. These stories give people hope, direction, and sometimes fear. In mythology, gods tell stories that explain human nature, the enigmas of life, and the complicated connections between people and the gods. This chapter discusses these gods' different areas and qualities, focusing on how they are connected to natural events, human feelings, and social norms. It provides a thorough and exciting look at the divine by breaking down the complicated stories of gods in mythology.

Zibelthiurdos

There is not a lot of information available about Zibelthiurdos. On the other hand, other people believe he was a Thracian god of storms and was responsible for sending lightning and thunder from the heavens to the earth. There are several similarities between these Thracian gods and the gods of the Greek pantheon, most prominently Zeus in this instance. In addition to being the king among the gods, Zeus was adored for his ability to control the strength of the heavens and the storm. There is a relationship between the names of Zibelthiurdos and Taranis, the thunder deity in Celtic mythology, and an etymological link between the two names. Both gods were thought to be personifications of the elements; in Thracian, 'thiurd' means to 'press down' or 'crash down,' and the word 'toranos' means 'thunder,' which is whence Taranis gets his name. The Thracians probably venerated the god of the storm with Zalmoxis or Gebeleizis as one of those 'Thracian Hero' gods.

Zibelthiurdos was a god of heaven, lightning, and rain in Thrace. His name is mainly known from the epigraphic monuments erected in his honour. Cicero's address against Pizon is the sole piece of ancient writing that is known to have referenced this deity. In that speech, he is referred to as

Jovi Vrii. This is the only known reference to him in ancient literature. According to Cicero, the barbarian temple dedicated to Jupiter Urius was the oldest and most revered of all of them; nonetheless, it was destroyed by invading troops, which led to the spread of diseases from which infected people never fully recovered. There is insufficient material to arrive at any definitive conclusions regarding his cult, the worship there, or the purposes it performs. Zibelthiurdos is pictured clutching a lightning bolt in his extended right hand, and to his right is an eagle with its wings spread out; this gives grounds to connect him with the ancient Greek god Zeus, Thunderer. The images that have been preserved give reason to make this connection.

Shrines of Zibelthiurdos have been discovered close to the town of Golemo Selo within the Kyustendil Region, inhabited by the Thracian Dentellets tribe. Other Zibelthiurdos temples have been discovered close to the village of Kapitan Dimitrievo in the Pazardzhik Province. His likeness was found on a relief that was excavated from Esquiline Hill. On the relief, he is shown beside Yambadula, a figure whose function is unknown.

Krali Marko

Legends and great songs about the mythical Krali Marko have been told and sung for hundreds of years. They changed over time and became increasingly detailed. He was the owner of a beautiful spotted horse. He met fairies, fought attackers and traitors, competed in heroic events, and freed thousands of slaves. And so it shouldn't be a surprise that many places in modern-day Bulgaria, Serbia, and Macedonia are named after him.

Behind the legendary Krali Marko is a real-life model, but by a strange mix of fate and irony, the honest Prince Marko possesses little time to spend with his legendary twin. It was terrible luck for Prince Marko that he was a relatively minor feudal king in the Balkans in the 1400s. At that time, the area was worn out from plagues, poor crops, religious fanaticism, and small fights that were breaking up Bulgaria, Serbia, and the Byzantine Empire, which used to be strong but was now weak. What used to be a small group of local forces was now a mix of big and small states and principalities, along with some rogue lords ready to take advantage of the situation.

There was a continuing Ottoman attack, and the

army was slowly taking over the area because it was so well organized. In 1371, both Serbian rulers, Vukašin and Uroš, died in this way. Soon, Prince Marko, who had a home in the town of Prilep and ruled in a part of what currently constitutes the Republic of Macedonia, became the heir to the Serbian throne. He never really became king. He instead swore allegiance to the Ottomans and stayed that way until the day he died, fighting against the sultan and other Christians in the conflict of Rovine.

The story of how an obedient Ottoman vassal turned into the fictional personification of Christian resistance against the Ottoman invasion will never be told. Most likely, it was just luck. On the other hand, the things that led to this change can be clearly described. They include the people's anger in the Balkans after the Ottoman invasion and their need to earn a hero to trust with their aspirations for independence. Another is the rise of national pride in the 18th and 19th centuries when artists and storytellers took Krali Marko from folk tales and epics and used him in modern performances, paintings, and books.

Bulgarians, Macedonians, and Serbs all say that Krali Marko is related to them, which is common in the area. On the other hand, the earliest records of the real Krali Marko are found in what is now the

Republic of Macedonia. The picture of the natural man has been kept safe in Marko's Monastery, located south of Skopje. The church wall painting of an aristocrat appears to be the last person on earth who could be a great hero, freeing slaves and protecting all of Christendom. He is dark, skinny, and troubled.

Prince Marko's home was Prilep, now a peaceful backwater town. However, the ruin of his fortress can still be seen on top of the rocks above the town. It's called Markovi Kuli, which means "Marko's Towers." The beautiful medieval Treskavec Monastery stands on a nearby hill. Even though there is no clear proof that Prince Marko was there, the building had been reconstructed in the 1400s, so he likely went there.

The abbey and the fortress are built on top of an old rock shrine. The shrine is a relic of a heathen cult common in the Balkans in prehistoric times and lasted until the sixth or seventh century AD. The connection makes you think: historians think that the legendary Krali Marko is just another form of the ancient Balkan hero who rode an animal and was worshipped in rock caves. Another reason people in the Balkans loved Krali Marko's stories in the Middle Ages is that they were based on real people, and stories about them were highly regarded. They just added new, accurate details to the stories.

In Bulgaria, stories about how Krali Marko came to show how a pagan custom and medieval history came together. They told me that Marko was Momchil Voyvoda's son. The king heard that Marko would one day take his throne, so he had him killed while he remained in the crib. His parents left Marko in the bush, and a nymph found him. She fed him milk, which gave him his magical abilities.

Bulgaria is full of the remains of old Thracian rock shrines that were thought to have been built by Krali Marko. Tradition says that the strange, big holes in some smooth rocks prove that Marko was there. Legends say that these are the marks of Marko and his horse, but scholars say they are the remains of ritual basins and rock tombs from long ago. So many places named Markova Stapka, Marko's Stage, Markov Kamak, Marko's Rock, or similar names used to be shrines. This list has many exciting places, such as the megalithic shrine in Tsarev Vrah peak within Rila, Markova Stapka close to Pernik, and the White Rock close to Marulevo village close to Blagoevgrad.

Many places where Krali Marko is said to have lived in legends are linked to bloody fights between him and his worst enemy, Musa Kesedzhiya, who is thought to represent the Ottoman invaders. This place is one of the most beautiful. It is the rocky tunnel of the Chernelka River near the village of Gortalovo. The story goes that Krali Marko and Musa clashed there for a single day and three nights. Krali Marko made a move with his Damascus sword, but Musa dodged it. The blow cut a massive rock in half. The chunk of stone is still there; part of the trail goes through the canyon.

Another story says that Krali Marko lived at the top of Botev Peak, the highest point in the Stara Planina. His chair, wheat field, and threshing platform were all turned to stone and can still be seen. Krali Marko is undoubtedly a hero, but some stories make him seem vain. Take the story of Marko and his sister, who was just as massive and powerful as he was. They planned to throw a stone across Maragidik Peak towards Stara Planina one day to see if they could do it the farthest. After throwing their stones, Marko got on his horse and saw who had won. His sister it was. Because he was so angry, the Hero left marks on the apartment rock with both his feet and the boots of his horse.

The two Roman piers near Pavlikeni are the subject of another story that shows Marko as a bad loser. They used to belong to the tomb of a Roman official in the area. However, over time, both the Roman and the tomb were lost. A story grew up about Krali Marko and a rival fighting over the affection of a local girl. The girl said she would marry the man who built the taller stone column. Marko won, but she picked his rival because she loved him more. Marko was furious and smashed his rival's column. People who live there still call it Markov Kamak.

CHAPTER 3: GODDESS

In mythology, goddesses are revered, often ethereal beings who play essential parts in the stories and spiritual beliefs of people worldwide. These holy female beings have unique traits ranging from caring and motherly to fierce and mysterious. Goddesses have stood for things like creation, fertility, wisdom, and protection in many countries and times.

They are revered as examples of the power and goodness of women, who shape fates, change the cycles of nature, and lead the way for people. In myths, legends, and religious stories, gods show us the many sides of being a woman, the mysteries of the universe, and the deep ties between humans and the divine. Myths about them often reflect societal ideals and ideas of what it means to be a woman, which gives us a glimpse into how men and women interacted in the past. This chapter explores mythology's fascinating world of goddesses, looking at their roles, traits, and meanings in different old cultures.

Bendis

Because Bendis is so ancient, her beginnings are obscured by the obscurity of time. Immigrants from Thrace transported her to Greece, and she quickly gained a significant following. Around the year 428 BCE, Bendis established an official state worship in the vicinity of Athens. It is possible that she was given to the Thracians by their neighbours, the Dacians. The Dacian kingdom was primarily located in what currently comprises Romania and Moldova. However, it also included parts of what is now Hungary, Bulgaria, and Ukraine. There is a possibility that Bendis comes from Scythian stock.

What we know about Bendis today is typically interpreted in terms of the Greek worldview. She was honoured, but at the same time, she was regarded as disreputable because she was a goddess of outsiders. She never forgot her Thracian heritage. The Greeks associated Bendis with Artemis or Hekate, even though she is even more strongly associated with the moon than any other.

Bendis can mean "moon" or "to bind." The word "binding" can refer to a marriage or shamanism; Bendis brings together several realms. She is the mother of the spirit that is currently without a name but is known as a Thracian Rider, Horseman, and Hero. Her reproductive abilities are so strong that she was able to give birth to her kid all by herself without the assistance of a male partner. Both the mother and the boy can be honoured in this way. After the spread of Christianity, venerating Mary and other local female saints took the place of honouring Bendis. Both the wilderness and the city are comfortable environments for Bendis. She embodies the ecstasy and ardour that is associated with the divine. Bendis is the very definition of lunar female power. She is asked to give birth to healthy children, have safe deliveries, be protected, have good health, and have good prosperity.

During that period, Bendis was characterized as donning a peaked Thracian cap, cloak, sleeveless tunic, and fox-skin boots; it is unknown whether or not she has upgraded her outfit since then. The nymphs, maenads, or satyrs whom Bendis is travelling with form an entourage for him. She has a very tight relationship with Artemis.

CHAPTER 4: MYTHICAL CREATURES

In mythology, mythical animals are imaginary and often out-of-this-world beings that live in the worlds of imagination and folklore. These fascinating animals are a mix of human, animal, and supernatural parts that push the limits of the natural world. They are essential parts of the myths and legends of many different cultures. They have traits and symbols that show how complicated human feelings, fears, and hopes are. Mythical animals like dragons, tricksters, and good spirits capture our imaginations and help us share cultural knowledge, tell stories, and express ourselves through art. In different cultures, these creatures show how the human mind can think of anything and how beliefs make up a complex web that has changed societies throughout history.

But these animals have been discussed extensively in traditions, legends, fables, writing, mythology, fairy-tale novels, myths, and other types of fiction. People who believe in realism say that stories about magical creatures have existed long before history became a science. People have a lot of different views and ideas about mythical beasts, which leads to many different theories about whether or not they exist. This part shows a massive group of exciting mythical creatures that make you want to know more. Also, this article has some interesting facts about the argument over whether mythical creatures exist and some ideas about where these fantastical animals might have come from.

Samodiva

Samodiva is the name given to an ethereal feminine wood nymph in the Bulgarian tradition. She has an otherworldly beauty, and she never seems to age. Her blond hair is long and very long, her bust is quite slim, and she has a tiny waist. Her eyes can beguile, dazzle, and even kill. When a man sees her, he cannot help but fall in love with her. A lady who witnesses a samodiva has the potential to end her own life because she is unable to bear the sight of so much beauty. The Samodivas dress in long white gowns, then shirts, and accessorize with a belt that is either rainbow-coloured or green. The source of their strength can be found within a white mantel, also known as a shadow. They enjoy riding deer and use snakes with their tails coiled around as reins. They also frequently carry bows and arrows with them. Suppose a hunter unintentionally takes the life of a samodiva's deer. In that case, the samodiva will either render the hunter blind or infect him with an illness that will eventually result in his death.

The homes of the wood nymphs can be found in the depths of dense forests, in the crooks of ancient trees, in caves, or in long-forgotten cabins next to springs, wells, or rivers. It is possible to see Samodivas from spring through fall. They spend the winter months in the legendary town of Zmeykovo, which sits on the planet's edge and is believed to be the abode of a wide variety of fantastical beasts. They only come out to roam the land at night and vanish when the sun rises because they are terrified of its rays. It's Samodivi. The Samodiva people, at dusk, make their way to fresh drinking water, where they strip down to their underwear, wash their garments, and then hang them out to dry under the moonlight. They keep a close eye on their laundry as it hangs out to dry since if a man were to steal their mantle, which is the source of their power, they would have to behave like ordinary women and follow the man. If this occurs, they can get married and have children. However, they will never be capable of being decent moms or homemakers, and they will always yearn for their independence.

Following the ritual washing of themselves and their garments, the samodivas congregate in one area and begin singing and dancing. It is common knowledge that the Samodiva people have the most exquisite music. At the same time, their dances are renowned as having the most grace. If a traveller arrives too late to observe the samodivas' dance, he will be lured to join them. He will dance alongside them from midnight until sunrise. When the day's rays appear, the nymphs flee quickly, leaving the traveller to pass out from tiredness and eventually perish. The samodivas have a deep appreciation for music, and they frequently abduct shepherds to force the shepherds to play the kaval for them as they dance. Many maintain that samodivas are Lamia's offspring. Some people believe that they are evil women who have passed away and are torn between heaven and hell.

In contrast, others believe that they are virgins who passed away before they ever knew a man. They celebrate Christian holidays, notably Easter, even though they are pagan creatures. In particular, they celebrate Christmas. They use blindness or execution as a form of punishment for anyone who does not observe the festivities.

It's not always the case that samodivas are dangerous. They will sometimes disguise themselves as regular working ladies and assist with the harvest. They would be of particular assistance to mothers who already have children. Suppose a man performs anything kind for a samodiva. In that case, he will become his patron or a sworn sister in exchange for their favour. It's not unheard of for a samodiva to fall in affection for someone else and give birth to his offspring, some of whom grow up becoming renowned saviours. Since Samodivas are woodland creatures, they have an extensive understanding of medicinal plants and remedies. On the other hand, they never voluntarily provide any of their information. The simplest way to get their expertise is to infiltrate one of their meetings and listen to their conversations.

The 13th century is when we find the earliest accounts of people believing that samodivas exist. It is generally agreed that the belief can be traced back to Thracian mythology. Many tales and poetry from Bulgarian folklore have been passed down through the generations and are dedicated to these enigmatic beauties.

Zmaj

In ancient mythology, the dragon constitutes one of the more well-known monsters, and numerous nations include a version of this mythical beast in their folklore. Dragons are considered to be emblems of power, strength, and good fortune in many of the countries that are located in East Asia. It is widely held that these beings are beneficent and control bodies that contain water, rain, and floods. In contrast, dragons are considered malicious creatures who are the personification of evil in Western European culture. The image of Saint George defeating the dragon is common in Western Europe's artwork. One of the legends of a dragon that is not very well known is that of a zmaj, a dragon that appears in Slavic folklore.

Depending on the dragon's gender, people in several Slavic countries attribute the creature a positive or negative connotation. For example, in Bulgarian folklore, male dragons are thought to guard crops, whilst female dragons are said to be hell-bent on destroying the products of man's labour. Male dragons are thought to breathe fire. In some regions of the Slavic globe, the dragon is regarded as a malevolent creature, just like in Western European cultures.

Zmey Gorynych is the name of a dragon-like creature that is feared in Russia and Ukraine. This dragon-like creature is a terrifying beast with multiple heads that spew fire. However, in Serbia, the zmaj is typically considered a good-natured being, similar to how dragons are viewed in East Asian cultures. It has been said that these beasts have "the head of a ram and the body of a seductive snake." It is supposed that these dragons guard the populace from the Ala, also known as the Azjada, which is a creature that is thought to bring terrible weather, including storms that ruin crops.

The Zmaj are rumoured to be capable of assuming various forms, even that of humans, in addition to their enormous strength and wisdom. One of these forms is said to be human. When they took on this shape, they were allowed to indulge in one of their favourite pastimes, the pursuit of women. It is believed that certain Zmaj become so involved in this practice that they forget to preserve agricultural grounds from adverse weather conditions. If inclement weather caused damage to the crops, the locals would congregate to drive the zmaj out of the homes of the local ladies. In the Serbian folk story titled The Tsarina Militza with the Zmaj of Yastrebatz, the lust of the zmaj towards mortal women is also an essential subject.

It is told that a zmaj of Yastrebatz paid a visit to the Tsarina Militza once a night for an entire year while she was in Yastrebatz. When her husband, the ruler of Serbia in the 14th century, Tsar Lazar, learns this, he instructs the tsarina to inquire of the zmaj as to whether or not he feared anyone other than God and whether or not there's a hero on this planet who is more heroic than himself. The Zmaj is duped into confessing the existence of the Zmaj-Despot Vook, who resided in a community in the plain of Sirmia known as Koopinova. The Zmaj is deceived into making this admission. The following day, the Tsar issued a summons to the Zmaj-Despot Vook, who travelled to Yastrebatz, where he eventually killed the zmaj who ruled the city.

It has been noted that the story of Zmaj-Despot Vook relies on an actual historical character known as Despot Vuk Brankovic. Despot Vuk Brankovic was a natural person who existed during the latter part of the 15th century and was considered a descendant of a dragon. How Vuk Brankovich was portrayed as a hero demonstrates how history or legend may be combined to serve the purposes of a ruler.

Other Serbian rulers besides Vuk have used the myth about the zmaj to boost their reputations.

Some additional kings assert that their forefathers were Zmaj. These include Stefan Lazarevi, son of Tsar Lazar and his successor, and Stojan Upi and Vasa Arapi, two prominent figures in the First Serbian Uprising, which took place at the beginning of the 19th century.

Some years ago, Serbia intended to cash in on the country's rich dragon history and turn the area into a tourist destination. The ideas were never put into effect. A tourist "dragon trail" would take visitors past various historical sites, such as churches, castles, and fortresses, all believed to have been frequented by the Zmaj. These days, a path like this may be seen in Serbia; it's called the "Paths of Dragons through Serbia" trail. The journey begins in the mountainous region of Fruka Gora in the country's north, continues via Belgrade, the nation's capital, and concludes at the fortified settlement of Markovo Kale in the country's south. This may assist in ensuring that the stories of the zmaj are passed on to subsequent generations, and it may also positively contribute to the tourism business in Serbia.

Kukeri: Scary Evil Spirit

Kukeri are Bulgarian men who dress in fancy clothes and do traditional practices to scare past evil spirits. This custom in Bulgaria has been around since the time of the Thracians and comes from the Thracians. In the Balkans and Greece, people follow customs that are very similar to each other. The outfits cover most of the human body and have animal masks made of decorated wood and big bells on the belt.

The Kukeri wear scary costumes and ring bells as they walk through towns around the start of Lent and New Year. People also think they will bring the village a good harvest, health, and happiness in the coming year. It is customary for the Kukeri to visit people at night so that "the rays of the sun wouldn't catch these individuals on the road."They often meet in the village centre to perform wildly and make people laugh after going around the village. Kukeri traditions differ in different parts of the world but are mostly the same.

Most people think the tradition has something to do with the Thracian Dionysos sect in Thracia and the surrounding area. Similar ceremonies are also prevalent in most of the Balkans. The word could come from the Proto-Slavic word kuka with the autonomous suffix added on or from the name of a pre-Slavic god. Another idea is that the word "kuker" comes from the Latin words "cuculla," which means "hood" or "cowl," or "cucurum," which means "to quiver." However, the practice happened hundreds of years before the Romans came to power.

In Greek-speaking Thrace, the figure is called Kalogeros, which means "rod-carrier" and can be shortened to cuci. In former Yugoslavia, it is called didi or didici; in Bulgaria, kuker or babushar; Pontic Anatolia, momogeros; and in North Macedonia, babari or mechkari. Many times in Romania, this persona is seen with a goat called a capra, turca, or breccia.

Kukeri is a goddess who represents fertility. In Bulgaria and Serbia, it is sometimes more than one god. When spring comes to Bulgaria, a traditional show happens after a scene from the folk theatre. A man dressed in sheep or goat skin, wearing a horned mask, and wearing a giant wooden phallus plays the part of Kuker. During the ritual, different bodily functions, such as sexual activity, are seen as representations of the god's holy marriage. The wife, who appears to be pregnant, plays out the pains that accompany birth. The Emperor and his company are among the many allegorical figures who participate in this ritual, which marks the start of work in the fields.

Capra comes from the Latin phrase "Capra," which means "goat." A headpiece resembling a halo was worn as a crown to represent the spiritual divine realm. Fur, feathers, and other animal parts on the outside of the body were connected to represent the world of nature. The idea that nature has both good and evil and that people are the link between the soul and nature meant it was time to honour the Spieth gods. As a show of support for the gods, some cultures drank human meat to quench their thirst for blood.

Lamya

The lamya is essentially a dragon in female form, albeit with a few key differences. The legend of the Lamya describes it as having three or nine heads, a body coated in yellow scales, and vicious teeth. According to specific accounts, it also possesses webbed wings and razor-sharp claws. In contrast to the typical dragon, the Lamya seldom harmed people, but it did blackmail them into giving it food. It is stated that a lamya had the power to halt rivers and lakes from flowing, causing droughts and compelling people to make sacrifices before it would enable rivers and lakes to resume their ordinary course of action. It is also said that courageous warriors or champions have battled lamyas. Yet, it was challenging to kill them because all of their heads must be cut in to kill the creature. The majority of people believe that they are aquatic creatures.

The lamya is a malevolent female dragon-like demon of drought in Bulgarian folklore. She is responsible for robbing the land of its fertility and preventing it from producing a harvest. Her most sworn adversary is the zmey, and whenever both of them come face to face, they engage in a fight of the elements that tear the heavens apart with lightning and thunder. There is also an exciting folk song based on Bulgarian mythology that tells the story of St. Ilya calling upon two zmeys, which are dragon archers armed with arrows of thunder, to search out and kill a lamya who is responsible for bringing famine and pestilence to the area.

There are fascinating similarities between the zmey and the Christian saint Ilya, revered in Bulgarian folklore as the lord of lightning and thunder. He pursues the malicious Lamya throughout the heavens on a blazing gold chariot while firing lightning bolts from his bow. It is believed that Saint Ilya was an incarnation of the Slavic god Perun, the god of lightning and thunder. In Slavic mythology, Perun fought his serpentine foe, Veles, using storms and lightning. St. Ilya has characteristics with several other pagan gods and goddesses as well. A fascinating connection between three distinct storm mythologies and their overlaying of one another

CHAPTER 5: LEGENDS

A legend is an old story or collection of stories about a person or place. The word "legend" meant a story about a holy person. According to legends, stories about supernatural beings, mythical creatures, or natural events are similar to folktales in what they say. However, legends are specific to a place or person and are told as historical facts.

Mythology studies stories that combine history, imagination, and traditional beliefs. These stories are called legends. In these stories, strange people, places, or things often cross the line between reality and the supernatural. Legends are told from generation to generation, becoming a big part of a community's identity and way of sharing stories. On the other hand, many local stories are just well-known stories linked to a specific person or place. Whether they are about heroic acts, the origins of natural landmarks, or the lives of famous people, these stories show what people value, what they hope for, and what makes life mysterious. Mythology's legends are a link between the everyday and the extraordinary. They remind people of their past and show how people are the same across time and countries.

Trifon Zarezan's Day

There is a story that when Trifon was just 17 years old, he treated the illness that had befallen the daughter of the Roman emperor Gordian. As a result, he gained renown and glory. They tried to convince him to renounce his Christian faith over the course of several years, but he resisted, and they brought the matter before the court. They gave him the death penalty, which was to be executed by beheading. As soon as they transported him outside the city, he faced east, prayed, and praised God for bestowing him the title of "martyr's wreath." During the course of his prayer, he bowed his head and passed away, freed from the torment of dying.

Another myth claims that when Trifon cut his vineyard, the Virgin Mary and Jesus Christ appeared to him and his sister. According to the tale, Mary was carrying Jesus at the time. She went to the prayer reading to celebrate her fortieth birthday. At her expense, Trifon laughed. She ignored the remark and, on the way back, when she came across his wife, she yelled at her to get bandages for her spouse in the field because he had cut his nose.

She then continued on her journey. The woman went without wasting any time. After learning why she is there, Trifon says, "How could You have cut it? Usually, hold the scissors downward, not up!" And to demonstrate to her that he was serious, he turned the scissors upside down and cut himself on the nose. Because of this, they refer to him as "Zarezan," on the icons, he is pictured with a pair of scissors in his hand.

On the saint's feast day, a ritualized chopping of the vines is carried out. Most of the rites and ceremonies performed on this day involve. The sole role that the ladies are expected to play is in the preparation of the feast. On this day, leavened bread is prepared for the rite. Rice is stuffed inside of a bird before it is roasted and served. Men from particular settlements in several regions of the country, most of which are located in Northern Bulgaria, get up early and travel to vineyards, where they take part in a ceremony called the "cutting." When the vines are pruned, wine is put on them immediately to encourage new growth and preserve fertility.

In some communities, a ritual known as "kicking of a fruitless tree" is done. This refers to kicking trees that did not produce any fruits. Because of this, the tree should finally start bearing fruit when all of this work is done. After completing those rites, males will set the table with the dishes prepared by their spouses. After that, a monarch is chosen, referred to as Trifon in various locations. A crown made of vine sticks is presented to the newly crowned monarch. He is being transported by one of the men on their hands. The king's duties are carried out during his first year in office. The following year saw the election of a new king.

Baba Marta

Baba Marta was the nickname of a legendary Bulgarian folklore character credited with ending the long, harsh winter and kicking off the season of spring. On March 1, Bulgarians celebrate the occasion that bears her name by exchanging martenitsi with one another and donning them throughout the day. Folklore associated with Baba Marta can also be found in the southeastern region of Serbia, specifically in the towns of Bosilegrad and Dimitrovgrad, both of which are home to a population that is predominantly Bulgarian in ethnicity. This is done as an allusion to a change in the weather that brings below-freezing temperatures following a spring break. There is a connection between the Romanian holiday of Martișor and Baba Marta.

On March 1, Bulgarians observe a tradition that dates back hundreds of years and trade martenitsi on holiday, known as the Day of the Baba Marta. A reminder that the warmer weather is just around the corner, the custom of bestowing upon one's friends a set of intertwined red and white strings is thought to bring good health and happiness throughout the year.

It is said that Baba Marta is a sassy old woman who always appears to be grouching at her two younger brothers in January and February and that the sun only shines when she smiles. Numerous variations of the Baba Marta story can be found in folklore. One story claims that on that day, she performs her pre-spring cleaning and then shakes the bed for the final time before the upcoming winter. All the feathers that fall out of it are said to fall to the ground like snow, making it the final snowfall of the year. This tale is also told in German traditions, for example, in the fable "Frau Holle", meaning Mother Hulda.

Martenitsi are bands or figurines of red and white colours representing health and happiness. They are believed to be an enticement against the influence of evil spirits. They are often worn around the hand or attached to clothing after being received as a gift from friends and relatives. People in the mountain communities adorn their homes, as well as their children and their animals kept as pets.

Initially, white was thought to represent man and the light solar zone. In later times, under the tutelage of Christian mythology, it came to signify chastity and virginity since white is the colour associated with Christ. The colour red is associated with women and health because it is a symbol of blood, pregnancy, and birth. In ancient times, brides wore red garments on their wedding day. The martenitsa can be found in various contexts and applications, ranging from the construction of packages to the attachment of strings to newborns' arms. In most cases, children compete to see who will receive the most.

People will wear martenitsa during a specific amount of time, and the conclusion of this time will typically coincide with the arrival of spring birds such as storks or swallows. Some people then fasten the martenitsa onto a tree, while others hide it beneath a rock; the following day, they look at what they discovered and make an educated judgment about the type of year that would be ahead of them. The custom of wearing a friendship bracelet that is supposed to bring good luck around one's wrist until it becomes worn out is similar to the folklore prevalent in several regions of Asia and South America. It is also similar to the German custom of hanging empty eggs from blossoming trees during Eastern folklore as the Persian custom of hanging fruit from trees during the middle of winter. Both of these customs originate in the Middle East.

Thracian Deities and Shrines

The Thracians lived in the Balkans for thousands of years, but they didn't like writing and didn't start their language. Because of this, we don't know much about their political past, religion, beliefs, or oral culture. It's hard to find sources that aren't written down because, like the Greeks, the Thracians didn't start drawing gods and heroes on graves, vessels, clothing, weapons, and harnesses until after the sixth century BC.

Because of this, much of what we understand about them originates from outside, not consistently solid sources: writers from ancient Greece, Rome, and Byzantium. Historical writers, chroniclers, poets, and scribes came from different cultures and sometimes lived hundreds of years after the occurrences and individuals they wrote about. This made it hard for them to be neutral. Because of this, both literal and figurative meanings were lost in translation, which makes it hard to tell the difference between fact and fiction in writings about the Thracians. Another problem with figuring out Thracian culture and history is that the people were notoriously divided. There were too many and too different Thracian tribes for there to be a single faith system that they all followed. There is a good chance that each tribe had its beliefs, traditions, and even gods.

Some things the Thracians left behind could help modern historians "read" their faith. These are the artefacts and shrines that have been found. But there is another risk in doing that. While studying the Thracian temples, historians with vivid imaginations often forget to use healthy scientific scepticism and begin to "see" faces of gods that don't exist, as well as "nuptial mattresses" and "devil's throats" all over. Many Thracian religious places, like Tatul and Perperikon at the Rhodope and Begliktash in a Strandzha, have been misunderstood in this way. In today's news, even natural things like the rocks that Buzovgrad are being sold as the work of the old Thracians. Any strangely shaped rock in the Rhodopes may be promoted as an authentic, massive, holy sculpture of turtles, snakes, or sharks.

But just because there aren't many written sources and it's hard to work with real places doesn't mean that historians don't know anything about the religious history of Thrace. A lot of beautiful and unique Thracian shrines can be found in Bulgaria. They are both fantastic and fun to see and learn about. The most critical Thrace shrines were built in the final stages of the Bronze Age. They were sometimes built in places where there was much religious activity in the past, like Belintash as well as Perperikon in a Rhodope. During the first millennium BC, these holy places did very well. Many weren't left until the fourth to sixth centuries when Christianity slowly took over.

These early chapels were built on steep, bare rocks in the Strandzha, Sakar, and Rhodope mountains. It's still easy to see why. They stand against the scenery, making it seem impossible, and can be seen far away.

Many of these rock shrines have a lot of channels, basins, pads, stairs, and nooks all over them. In Thrace, the Great Goddess was thought to have formed the world in her stone uterus when she got pregnant by her son and lover, the Great God, who is also a sun symbol. The almost anthropomorphic shapes of the rocks in these shrines, like vulva-shaped crevices and rocks that look like straight phalluses, support this theory. In their stories, ancient writers have kept the idea of an essential and well-known Thracian sanctuary alive. In the lands ruled by Bessi, the Oracle for Dionysus lived. Its priestesses could accurately tell the future, including how people like Alexander the Mighty and Augustus became emperors of Rome. Where the oracle is, however, is still a secret.

It is also hard to figure out which gods are worshipped in Thrace's shrines. The Greeks told us about ancient Thracian gods and goddesses, like Zalmoxis, Cotyto, and Bendis. The Thracians were also said to have worshipped Dionysos, Artemis, Apollo, and Hermes. The unknown Thracian God Steed Popular is well-known, mostly on tribute tablets. There is still some doubt whether these gods weren't just different forms of the Big Goddess and the Great God. Thracian art has an image of a female goddess that shows up repeatedly. This was likely the Thracian Great, the Goddess, who made the world and controlled it. She is shown in many places, such as the jugs and bowls in the Rogozen Treasure, the paintings and sculptures in the Sveshtari Tomb, the gold rings, and the murals and sculptures in the Kazanlak Tomb.

Thracian kings were allowed to be in charge of the government by the Great Goddess. In Thrace, the king or chief of the group was also the state's prominent priest. People saw him as the Great God come to life on earth, and he would marry the Great Goddess in ceremonies that were meant to be symbolic.

The ancient Greeks thought that everyone would

spend eternity as a shadow in the sad land of Hades after they died. But the Thracians thought there was life after death. Herodotus says that some groups were so happy when someone died that their wives would start fighting over who would be cremated along with the person. Noble Thracians, who were said to follow Orpheus's mystic beliefs, were made gods after dying. Because of this, many sites have some kind of grave or tomb, like a dolmen, a rock tomb, or a large tomb. These were not just graves; they additionally served as places of worship for the gods whose bodies were buried there.

Massive tombs were sometimes used as shrines and many clues point in this direction. The vast tombs all have passageways, suggesting they were visited often. Some of them had very fancy fronts, which made it look like they had been constructed to be a sight for the existents who would do strange rituals inside the rooms. The stone steps of these tombs are worn down from being walked on by so many people. The bodies of regular killings are kept safe within and close to the tombs.

Archaeologists haven't found many artefacts to study in rock sanctuaries because they are complex and empty, and people have been looking for wealth there for hundreds of years. The most common things in Thrace shrines are whole or broken pottery, tools and weapons, animal bones, and burned clay to the buildings that the priests and visitors used as light. Not all of these creations were created just for the rituals. For example, idols, amulets, and tokens for religious games were all made to scale. Still, more were things that people used daily, like millstones and cash, jewellery and weapons, sickles and knives, pegs and loom weights, and more. Some of these gifts were broken or scratched up, especially as if they should be slain for the benefit of the gods.

Some shrines have temples, but most in Thrace's central region have not been positively recognized. The only ones found are in the Greek colonies on the Black Sea coast. Thracian shrines have been found on Plovdiv's Nebet Tepe Hill, in the sunken city of Seuthopolis near Kazanlak, Cabyle near Yambol, and other places. An engraving at Seuthopolis says that the city included a shrine to Dionysus and a temple to the Great Gods. In Cabyle, there was a temple to Artemis Phosphoros, also known as the Light-Bearer, a form of the Thracians' Great Goddess. But it's possible that there were more churches. An everyday find in inland Thrace would support this idea. It is about the altars, made of clay and shaped like square or rectangular pads with many geometric patterns. One can find these in towns and shrines and the piles of large tombs and graves.

Another kind of shrine popped up between the sixth and 1st centuries BC. They were temples made out of holes dug in the ground. These became the most popular religious places in the middle part of Thrace. The pits were of different sizes and forms, like pears, beehives, and casks. They were both cone-shaped and cylindrical. Each was about one to two meters deep and full of broken ceramics, animal bones, ashes, and hot rocks. Parts or whole human bodies have been found in about 1% to 2% of these. Some of the people who were thrown into the pits were still living when they were put there, which supports the idea that they were killed and sacrificed to the Thrace gods.

Once more, Herodotus throws light on what the archaeologists have found. He said that when some Thracian groups thought the God Zalmoxis needed to pay more attention to their prayers, they would pound spears into the ground, pick the most muscular man, and throw him with the blades. They would send their words to the gods while he was dying. Many experts think that the pit altars were part of the cult of the most powerful Goddess. The holes stood for her womb and gave her a link to the spirits from the Underworld and fertility.

The Thracians also worshipped streams and running water. They made many shrines near water, but most were destroyed when dams and reservoirs were built in the 20th century. Some of these are the places in Bratsigovo and Ognyanovo, which are close to Pazardzhik. Some minor Thracian artefacts have been kept safe in later Roman shrines by holy springs. One example is the temple for the fairies at Kasnakovo, close to Dimitrovgrad. The only Thracian shrine by a holy spring that has been studied in depth is the one in Sboryanovo, which is beneath the Ottoman Demir Baba tekke.

As Christianity spread across the Balkans, people forgot about the Thracian gods and their shrines. But they didn't go away. For example, in Pliska, Madara, and Montana, churches were built on the remains of several pagan sites. Both Christians and Muslims now revere many Thracian sites. The old gods also changed, becoming part of local legends and affecting the Christian saints.

When Christianity came to Thrace in the fourth millennium, some old shrines were lost, but others were still used by lines of people who worshipped their gods and saints. Many cave springs on the Strandzha mountain were holy for the Thracians and have since been transformed into chapels for Christian saints. There is such a site in the Strandzha, but an archaeological study has not yet been done. People think that the water source in the small cave can heal them. Indipasha is full of visitors on the Sunday following Easter, which suggests a link between paganism and Christianity.

One Last Thing...

We're glad you're interested in this book. I hope you have fun reading it as I did writing it. This book is for all those people with big eyes and many questions. I hope your interest in these old stories will help them live on forever.

I have always considered your insightful reviews to be an excellent source of viewpoints on books, and it would be an honour for me if you would review This book. Your perceptive analysis and comments would not only be of great use to me as an author, but they would also serve potential readers in understanding the issues and traits covered in the book. I am very aware of the constraints imposed by the little time you have at your disposal; thus, I ask that you please consider the following request.

I am thankful that you considered what I had to say about the book and took the time to do so. I would be more than happy to provide some further input and ideas. Please do not hesitate to contact me. If you would like to give feedback on my book, you only need to navigate to the reviews part of my content. You will notice a sizable button that asks you to "Write a customer review." Select that link, and you will be taken to the appropriate page.

Printed in Great Britain
by Amazon

41188328R00036